The ULTIMATE financial Planner

A 365 DAY JOURNEY TO FINANCIAL FREEDOM

SELENA GIBBONS

IBG PUBLICATIONS
Putting the POWER in your pen!

Published by I.B.G. Publications, LLC, a Power to Wealth Company
Web address: www.ibgpublications.com
admin@ibgpublications.com / 904-419-9810

IBG Publications, LLC, Jacksonville, FL
ISBN #: 978-1-956266-12-2

Gibbons, Selena
The Ultimate Financial Planner: A 365 Day Journey to Financial Freedom
www.selenagibbons.com

Printed in the United States of America.

THIS FINANCIAL PLANNER
BELONGS TO:

I DESERVE AND
EXPECT
FINANCIAL
ABUNDANCE.
WWW.PossibleFinance.Com

52 Week Saving CHALLENGE

Week	Deposit	Balance	Done	Week	Deposit	Balance	Done
1	$1.00	$1.00	____	27	$27.00	$378.00	____
2	$2.00	$3.00	____	28	$28.00	$406.00	____
3	$3.00	$6.00	____	29	$29.00	$435.00	____
4	$4.00	$10.00	____	30	$30.00	$465.00	____
5	$5.00	$15.00	____	31	$31.00	$496.00	____
6	$6.00	$21.00	____	32	$32.00	$528.00	____
7	$7.00	$28.00	____	33	$33.00	$561.00	____
8	$8.00	$36.00	____	34	$34.00	$595.00	____
9	$9.00	$45.00	____	35	$35.00	$630.00	____
10	$10.00	$55.00	____	36	$36.00	$666.00	____
11	$11.00	$66.00	____	37	$37.00	$703.00	____
12	$12.00	$78.00	____	38	$38.00	$741.00	____
13	$13.00	$91.00	____	39	$39.00	$780.00	____
14	$14.00	$105.00	____	40	$40.00	$820.00	____
15	$15.00	$120.00	____	41	$41.00	$861.00	____
16	$16.00	$136.00	____	42	$42.00	$903.00	____
17	$17.00	$153.00	____	43	$43.00	$946.00	____
18	$18.00	$171.00	____	44	$44.00	$990.00	____
19	$19.00	$190.00	____	45	$45.00	$1035.00	____
20	$20.00	$219.00	____	46	$46.00	$1081.00	____
21	$21.00	$231.00	____	47	$47.00	$1128.00	____
22	$22.00	$253.00	____	48	$48.00	$1176.00	____
23	$23.00	$276.00	____	49	$49.00	$1225.00	____
24	$24.00	$300.00	____	50	$50.00	$1275.00	____
25	$25.00	$325.00	____	51	$51.00	$1326.00	____
26	$26.00	$351.00	____	52	$52.00	$1378.00	____

Grand Total: ______________________

JANUARY

MONTH AT A GLANCE

"FINANCIAL FREEDOM IS A LIFESTYLE."

SUN	MON	TUE	WED	THURS	FRI	SAT

Notes:

Personal Vision Board

Visualize Your Month

Date:

Goals:

Priorities:

Financial:

To Buy:

Notes:

Weekly Goals Checklist

JANUARY

List the steps you will take to complete your goal. Check off each step once complete.

WEEKLY FOCUS

Sunday

- [ ] ______
- [ ] ______
- [ ] ______
- [ ] ______
- [ ] ______

Monday

- [ ] ______
- [ ] ______
- [ ] ______
- [ ] ______
- [ ] ______

Tuesday

- [ ] ______
- [ ] ______
- [ ] ______
- [ ] ______
- [ ] ______

Wednesday

- [ ] ______
- [ ] ______
- [ ] ______
- [ ] ______
- [ ] ______

Thursday

- [ ] ______
- [ ] ______
- [ ] ______
- [ ] ______
- [ ] ______

Friday

- [ ] ______
- [ ] ______
- [ ] ______
- [ ] ______
- [ ] ______

Saturday

- [ ] ______
- [ ] ______
- [ ] ______
- [ ] ______
- [ ] ______

WEEK #1

My Monthly DEBT LIST

Extra Payment To Put Towards Debt: ______________________

Priority	Debt Name	Total Owed	Min. Monthly Pmt.	Extra Monthly Pmt.	Months To Pay Off

MONTHLY BILL TRACKER

Bill	Amount	Due Date	Paid

MONTHLY BUDGET SHEET

ESTIMATED BUDGET -

PRIORITIES -

BUDGET GOALS -

WAYS TO SAVE -

DESCRIPTION	BUDGET	SPENT

DESCRIPTION	BUDGET	SPENT

This week's affirmation...

I AM CAPABLE OF OVERCOMING ANY MONEY OBSTACLES THAT MAY STAND IN MY WAY.

Weekly Goals Checklist

JANUARY

List the steps you will take to complete your goal. Check off each step once complete.

WEEKLY FOCUS

Sunday

- ☐ ____
- ☐ ____
- ☐ ____
- ☐ ____
- ☐ ____

Monday

- ☐ ____
- ☐ ____
- ☐ ____
- ☐ ____
- ☐ ____

Tuesday

- ☐ ____
- ☐ ____
- ☐ ____
- ☐ ____
- ☐ ____

Wednesday

- ☐ ____
- ☐ ____
- ☐ ____
- ☐ ____
- ☐ ____

Thursday

- ☐ ____
- ☐ ____
- ☐ ____
- ☐ ____
- ☐ ____

Friday

- ☐ ____
- ☐ ____
- ☐ ____
- ☐ ____
- ☐ ____

Saturday

- ☐ ____
- ☐ ____
- ☐ ____
- ☐ ____
- ☐ ____

WEEK #2

This week's affirmation...
I CAN CONQUER
MY MONEY GOALS.

Weekly Goals Checklist

JANUARY

List the steps you will take to complete your goal. Check off each step once complete.

WEEKLY FOCUS

Sunday

- ☐ ____
- ☐ ____
- ☐ ____
- ☐ ____
- ☐ ____

Monday

- ☐ ____
- ☐ ____
- ☐ ____
- ☐ ____
- ☐ ____

Tuesday

- ☐ ____
- ☐ ____
- ☐ ____
- ☐ ____
- ☐ ____

Wednesday

- ☐ ____
- ☐ ____
- ☐ ____
- ☐ ____
- ☐ ____

Thursday

- ☐ ____
- ☐ ____
- ☐ ____
- ☐ ____
- ☐ ____

Friday

- ☐ ____
- ☐ ____
- ☐ ____
- ☐ ____
- ☐ ____

Saturday

- ☐ ____
- ☐ ____
- ☐ ____
- ☐ ____
- ☐ ____

WEEK #3

This week's affirmation...
TODAY I COMMIT TO
LIVING MY
FINANCIAL DREAMS.

Weekly Goals Checklist

JANUARY

List the steps you will take to complete your goal. Check off each step once complete.

WEEKLY FOCUS

Sunday

- [ ] ______
- [ ] ______
- [ ] ______
- [ ] ______
- [ ] ______

Monday

- [ ] ______
- [ ] ______
- [ ] ______
- [ ] ______
- [ ] ______

Tuesday

- [ ] ______
- [ ] ______
- [ ] ______
- [ ] ______
- [ ] ______

Wednesday

- [ ] ______
- [ ] ______
- [ ] ______
- [ ] ______
- [ ] ______

Thursday

- [ ] ______
- [ ] ______
- [ ] ______
- [ ] ______
- [ ] ______

Friday

- [ ] ______
- [ ] ______
- [ ] ______
- [ ] ______
- [ ] ______

Saturday

- [ ] ______
- [ ] ______
- [ ] ______
- [ ] ______
- [ ] ______

WEEK #4

This week's affirmation…

I WANT BETTER CREDIT, AND THAT'S OK!

FEBRUARY

MONTH AT A GLANCE

"I AM PASSIONATE ABOUT MY GOALS AND NOTHING CAN STOP ME."

SUN	MON	TUE	WED	THURS	FRI	SAT

Notes:

Personal Vision Board

Visualize Your Month

Date:

Goals:

Priorities:

Financial:

To Buy:

Notes:

Weekly Goals Checklist

FEBRUARY

List the steps you will take to complete your goal. Check off each step once complete.

WEEKLY FOCUS

Sunday

- [ ] ______
- [ ] ______
- [ ] ______
- [ ] ______
- [ ] ______

Monday

- [ ] ______
- [ ] ______
- [ ] ______
- [ ] ______
- [ ] ______

Tuesday

- [ ] ______
- [ ] ______
- [ ] ______
- [ ] ______
- [ ] ______

Wednesday

- [ ] ______
- [ ] ______
- [ ] ______
- [ ] ______
- [ ] ______

Thursday

- [ ] ______
- [ ] ______
- [ ] ______
- [ ] ______
- [ ] ______

Friday

- [ ] ______
- [ ] ______
- [ ] ______
- [ ] ______
- [ ] ______

Saturday

- [ ] ______
- [ ] ______
- [ ] ______
- [ ] ______
- [ ] ______

WEEK #1

My Monthly DEBT LIST

Extra Payment To Put Towards Debt: ______________________________

Priority	Debt Name	Total Owed	Min. Monthly Pmt.	Extra Monthly Pmt.	Months To Pay Off

MONTHLY BILL TRACKER

Bill	Amount	Due Date	Paid

MONTHLY BUDGET SHEET

ESTIMATED BUDGET -

PRIORITIES -

BUDGET GOALS -

WAYS TO SAVE -

DESCRIPTION	BUDGET	SPENT

DESCRIPTION	BUDGET	SPENT

This week's affirmation...
MY LIFE IS FILLED WITH
HEALTH AND WEALTH.

Weekly Goals Checklist

FEBRUARY

List the steps you will take to complete your goal. Check off each step once complete.

WEEKLY FOCUS

Sunday

- [ ] ______
- [ ] ______
- [ ] ______
- [ ] ______
- [ ] ______

Monday

- [ ] ______
- [ ] ______
- [ ] ______
- [ ] ______
- [ ] ______

Tuesday

- [ ] ______
- [ ] ______
- [ ] ______
- [ ] ______
- [ ] ______

Wednesday

- [ ] ______
- [ ] ______
- [ ] ______
- [ ] ______
- [ ] ______

Thursday

- [ ] ______
- [ ] ______
- [ ] ______
- [ ] ______
- [ ] ______

Friday

- [ ] ______
- [ ] ______
- [ ] ______
- [ ] ______
- [ ] ______

Saturday

- [ ] ______
- [ ] ______
- [ ] ______
- [ ] ______
- [ ] ______

WEEK #2

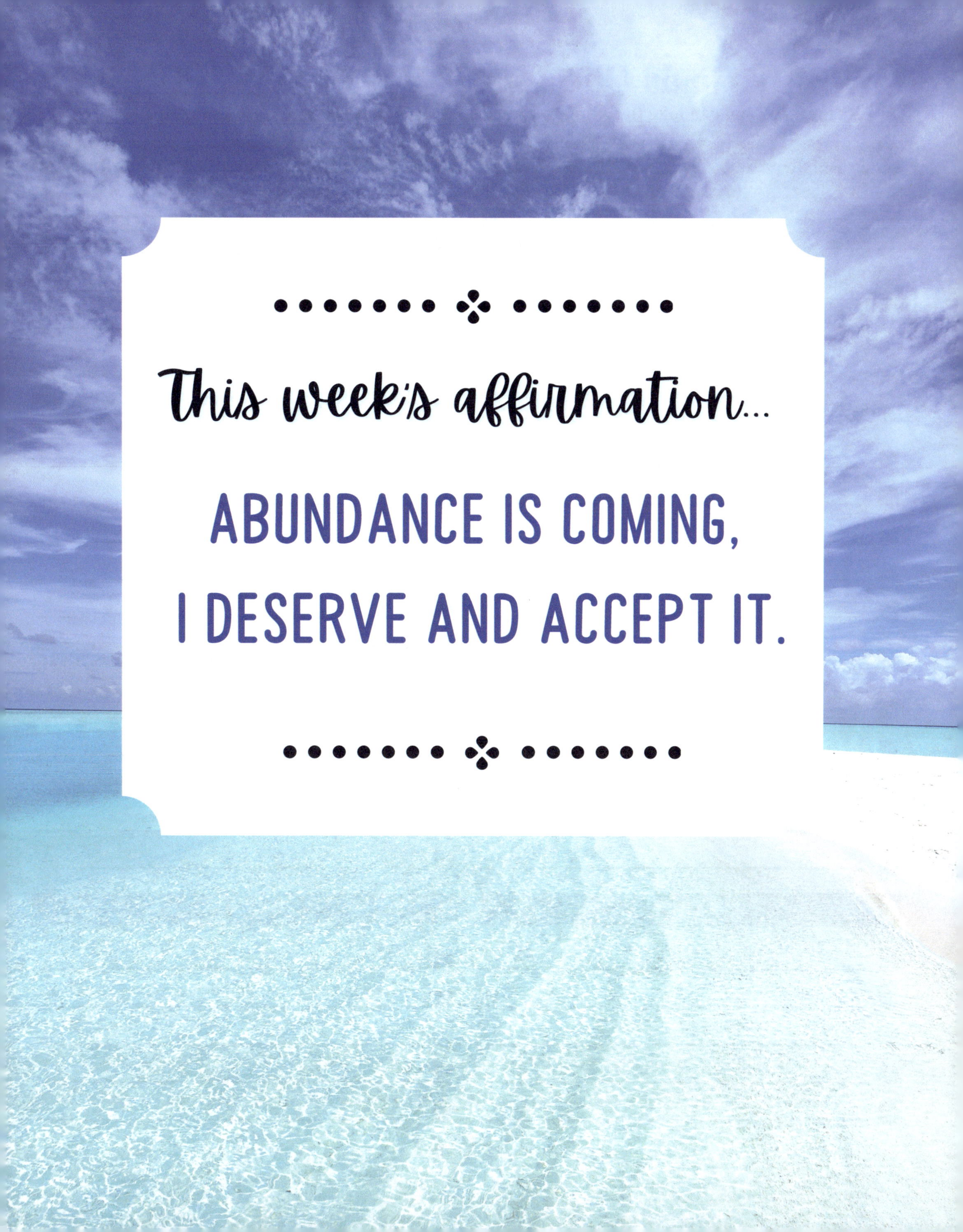

This week's affirmation...

ABUNDANCE IS COMING,
I DESERVE AND ACCEPT IT.

Weekly Goals Checklist

FEBRUARY

List the steps you will take to complete your goal. Check off each step once complete.

WEEKLY FOCUS

Sunday

- [ ] ______
- [ ] ______
- [ ] ______
- [ ] ______
- [ ] ______

Monday

- [ ] ______
- [ ] ______
- [ ] ______
- [ ] ______
- [ ] ______

Tuesday

- [ ] ______
- [ ] ______
- [ ] ______
- [ ] ______
- [ ] ______

Wednesday

- [ ] ______
- [ ] ______
- [ ] ______
- [ ] ______
- [ ] ______

Thursday

- [ ] ______
- [ ] ______
- [ ] ______
- [ ] ______
- [ ] ______

Friday

- [ ] ______
- [ ] ______
- [ ] ______
- [ ] ______
- [ ] ______

Saturday

- [ ] ______
- [ ] ______
- [ ] ______
- [ ] ______
- [ ] ______

WEEK #3

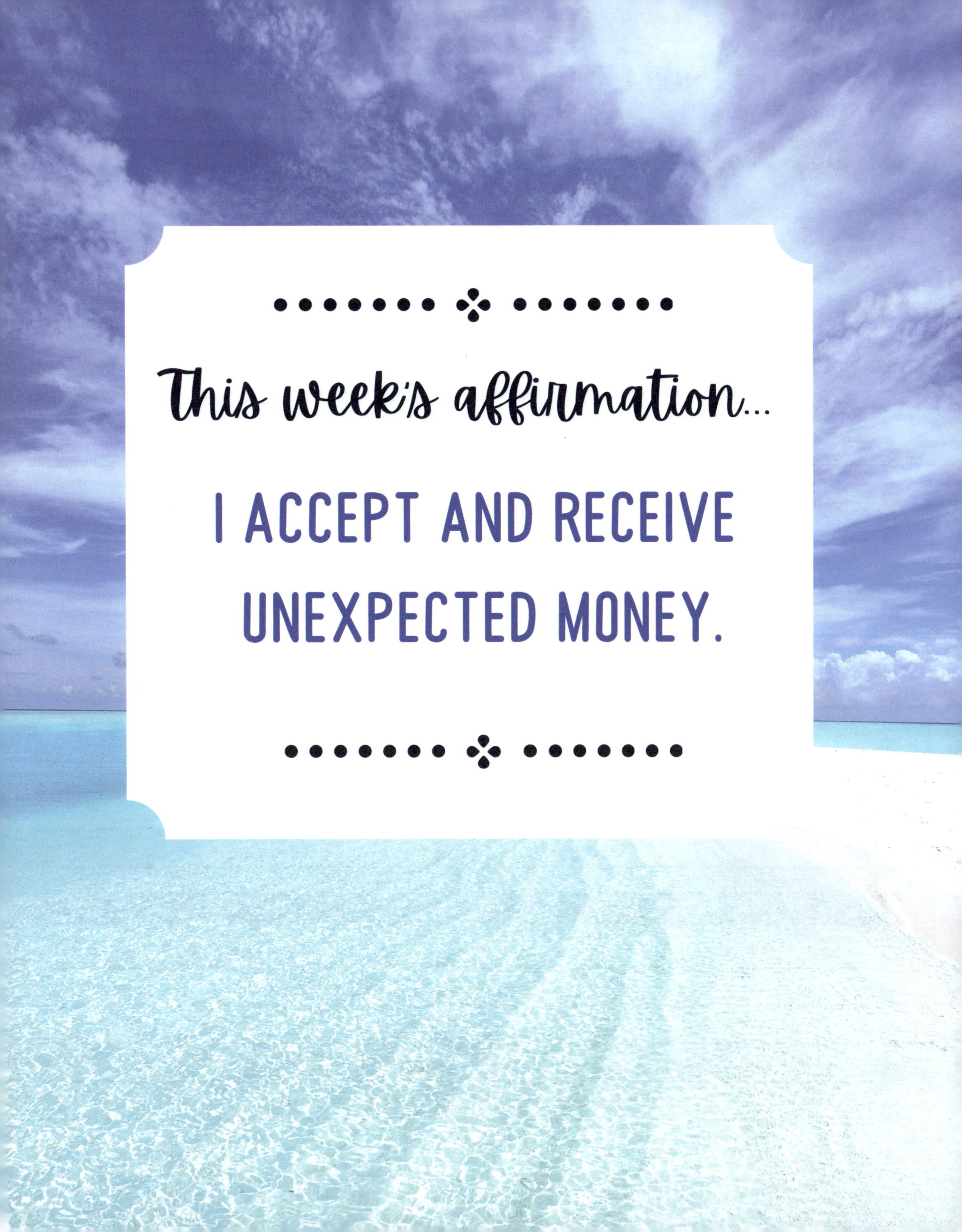

This week's affirmation...

I ACCEPT AND RECEIVE UNEXPECTED MONEY.

Weekly Goals Checklist

FEBRUARY

List the steps you will take to complete your goal. Check off each step once complete.

WEEKLY FOCUS

Sunday

Monday

Tuesday

Wednesday

Thursday

Friday

Saturday

WEEK #4

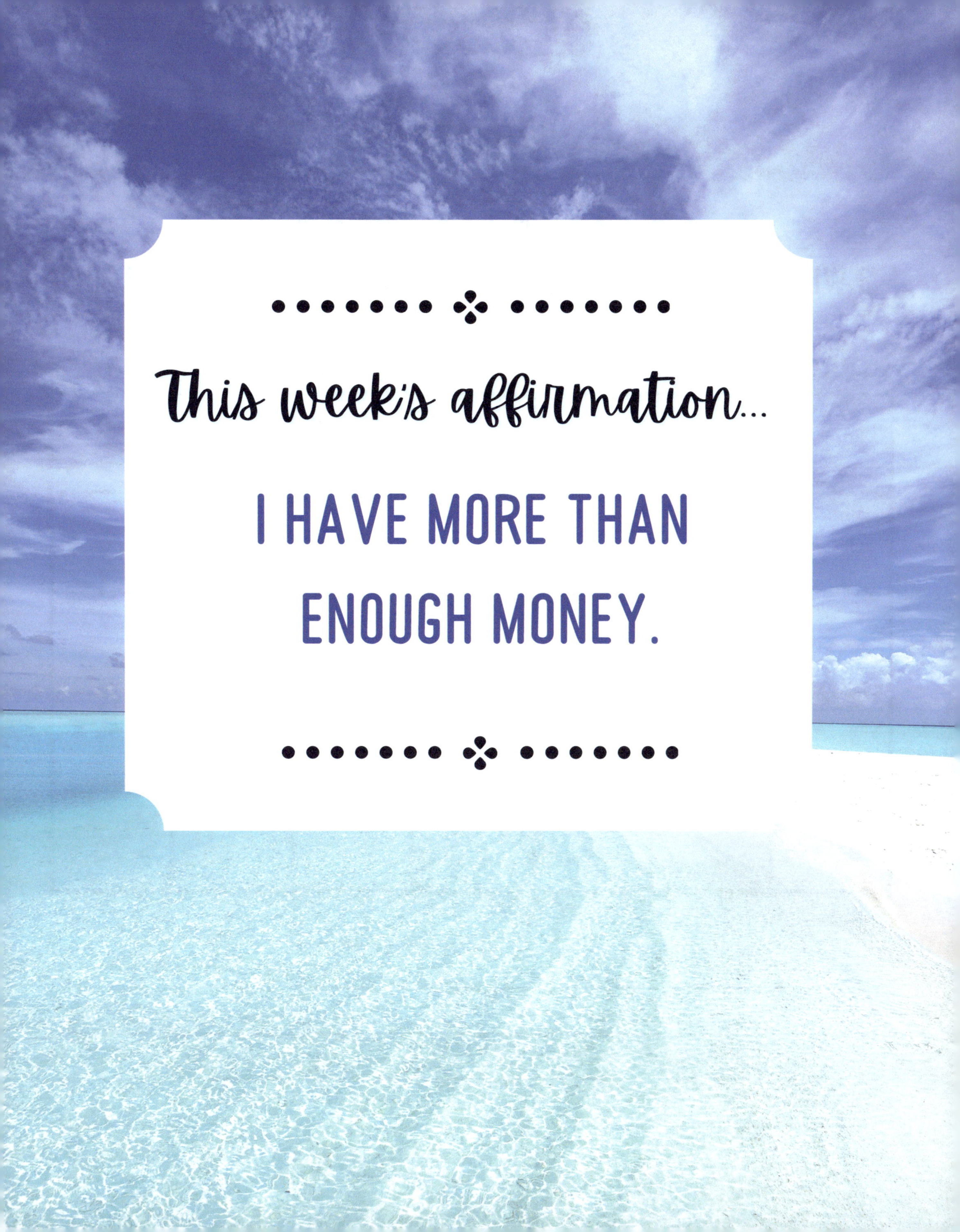

This week's affirmation...

I HAVE MORE THAN ENOUGH MONEY.

MARCH

MONTH AT A GLANCE

"I WILL WORK HARD TO ACHIEVE EVERY FINANCIAL GOAL I SET."

SUN	MON	TUE	WED	THURS	FRI	SAT

Notes:

Personal Vision Board

Date:

Visualize Your Month

Goals:

Financial:

To Buy:

Priorities:

Notes:

Weekly Goals Checklist

MARCH

List the steps you will take to complete your goal. Check off each step once complete.

WEEKLY FOCUS

Sunday

- [ ] ____
- [ ] ____
- [ ] ____
- [ ] ____
- [ ] ____

Monday

- [ ] ____
- [ ] ____
- [ ] ____
- [ ] ____
- [ ] ____

Tuesday

- [ ] ____
- [ ] ____
- [ ] ____
- [ ] ____
- [ ] ____

Wednesday

- [ ] ____
- [ ] ____
- [ ] ____
- [ ] ____
- [ ] ____

Thursday

- [ ] ____
- [ ] ____
- [ ] ____
- [ ] ____
- [ ] ____

Friday

- [ ] ____
- [ ] ____
- [ ] ____
- [ ] ____
- [ ] ____

Saturday

- [ ] ____
- [ ] ____
- [ ] ____
- [ ] ____
- [ ] ____

WEEK #1

My Monthly DEBT LIST

Extra Payment To Put Towards Debt: ______________________

Priority	Debt Name	Total Owed	Min. Monthly Pmt.	Extra Monthly Pmt.	Months To Pay Off

MONTHLY BILL TRACKER

Bill	Amount	Due Date	Paid

MONTHLY BUDGET SHEET

ESTIMATED BUDGET -

PRIORITIES -

BUDGET GOALS -

WAYS TO SAVE -

DESCRIPTION	BUDGET	SPENT

DESCRIPTION	BUDGET	SPENT

This week's affirmation...

I AM ALWAYS DISCOVERING NEW SOURCES OF INCOME.

Weekly Goals Checklist

MARCH

List the steps you will take to complete your goal. Check off each step once complete.

WEEKLY FOCUS

Sunday

- [ ] ____
- [ ] ____
- [ ] ____
- [ ] ____
- [ ] ____

Monday

- [ ] ____
- [ ] ____
- [ ] ____
- [ ] ____
- [ ] ____

Tuesday

- [ ] ____
- [ ] ____
- [ ] ____
- [ ] ____
- [ ] ____

Wednesday

- [ ] ____
- [ ] ____
- [ ] ____
- [ ] ____
- [ ] ____

Thursday

- [ ] ____
- [ ] ____
- [ ] ____
- [ ] ____
- [ ] ____

Friday

- [ ] ____
- [ ] ____
- [ ] ____
- [ ] ____
- [ ] ____

Saturday

- [ ] ____
- [ ] ____
- [ ] ____
- [ ] ____
- [ ] ____

WEEK #2

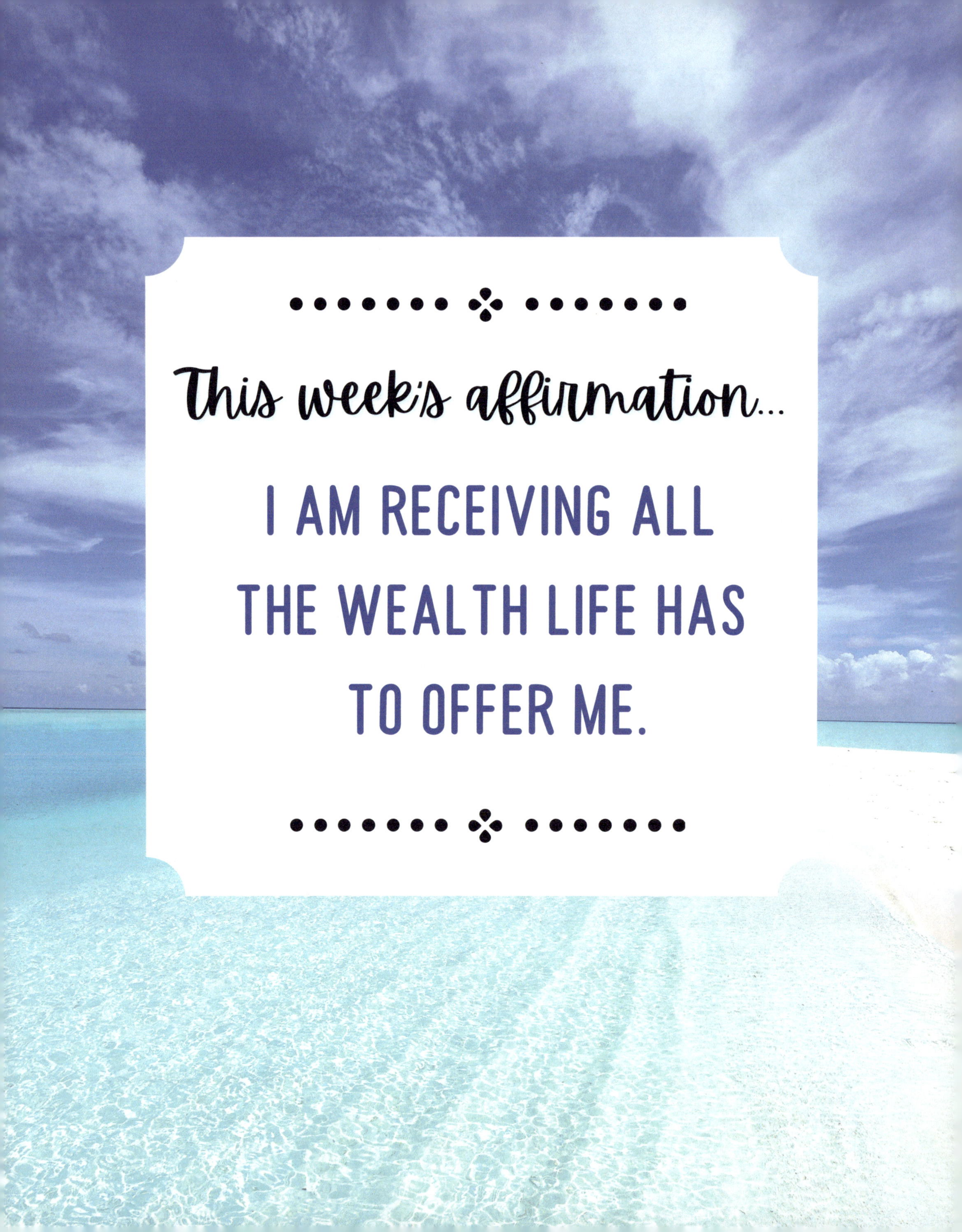

This week's affirmation...

I AM RECEIVING ALL
THE WEALTH LIFE HAS
TO OFFER ME.

Weekly Goals Checklist

MARCH

List the steps you will take to complete your goal. Check off each step once complete.

WEEKLY FOCUS

Sunday

- [ ] ______
- [ ] ______
- [ ] ______
- [ ] ______
- [ ] ______

Monday

- [ ] ______
- [ ] ______
- [ ] ______
- [ ] ______
- [ ] ______

Tuesday

- [ ] ______
- [ ] ______
- [ ] ______
- [ ] ______
- [ ] ______

Wednesday

- [ ] ______
- [ ] ______
- [ ] ______
- [ ] ______
- [ ] ______

Thursday

- [ ] ______
- [ ] ______
- [ ] ______
- [ ] ______
- [ ] ______

Friday

- [ ] ______
- [ ] ______
- [ ] ______
- [ ] ______
- [ ] ______

Saturday

- [ ] ______
- [ ] ______
- [ ] ______
- [ ] ______
- [ ] ______

WEEK #3

This week's affirmation...

MY WEALTH STATUS IS CHANGING

Weekly Goals Checklist

MARCH

List the steps you will take to complete your goal. Check off each step once complete.

WEEKLY FOCUS	Sunday
	☐ ______
	☐ ______
	☐ ______
	☐ ______
	☐ ______

Monday	Tuesday
☐ ______	☐ ______
☐ ______	☐ ______
☐ ______	☐ ______
☐ ______	☐ ______
☐ ______	☐ ______

Wednesday	Thursday
☐ ______	☐ ______
☐ ______	☐ ______
☐ ______	☐ ______
☐ ______	☐ ______
☐ ______	☐ ______

Friday	Saturday
☐ ______	☐ ______
☐ ______	☐ ______
☐ ______	☐ ______
☐ ______	☐ ______
☐ ______	☐ ______

WEEK #4

This week's affirmation...

I HAVE A WEALTHY MINDSET.

APRIL

MONTH AT A GLANCE

"I WILL BE PATIENT IN MY FINANCIAL JOUURNEY."

SUN	MON	TUE	WED	THURS	FRI	SAT

Notes:

Personal Vision Board

Visualize Your Month

Date:

Goals:

Priorities:

Financial:

To Buy:

Notes:

Weekly Goals Checklist

APRIL

List the steps you will take to complete your goal. Check off each step once complete.

WEEKLY FOCUS

Sunday

- [ ] ______
- [ ] ______
- [ ] ______
- [ ] ______
- [ ] ______

Monday

- [ ] ______
- [ ] ______
- [ ] ______
- [ ] ______
- [ ] ______

Tuesday

- [ ] ______
- [ ] ______
- [ ] ______
- [ ] ______
- [ ] ______

Wednesday

- [ ] ______
- [ ] ______
- [ ] ______
- [ ] ______
- [ ] ______

Thursday

- [ ] ______
- [ ] ______
- [ ] ______
- [ ] ______
- [ ] ______

Friday

- [ ] ______
- [ ] ______
- [ ] ______
- [ ] ______
- [ ] ______

Saturday

- [ ] ______
- [ ] ______
- [ ] ______
- [ ] ______
- [ ] ______

WEEK #1

My Monthly DEBT LIST

Extra Payment To Put Towards Debt: ______________________________

Priority	Debt Name	Total Owed	Min. Monthly Pmt.	Extra Monthly Pmt.	Months To Pay Off

MONTHLY BILL TRACKER

Bill	Amount	Due Date	Paid

MONTHLY BUDGET SHEET

ESTIMATED BUDGET -

PRIORITIES -

BUDGET GOALS -

WAYS TO SAVE -

DESCRIPTION	BUDGET	SPENT

DESCRIPTION	BUDGET	SPENT

This week's affirmation...

I WON'T LET WHERE MY FINANCIAL SITUATION IS NOW DISTRACT ME FROM MY FUTURE.

Weekly Goals Checklist

APRIL

List the steps you will take to complete your goal. Check off each step once complete.

WEEKLY FOCUS

Sunday

- [ ] ______
- [ ] ______
- [ ] ______
- [ ] ______
- [ ] ______

Monday

- [ ] ______
- [ ] ______
- [ ] ______
- [ ] ______
- [ ] ______

Tuesday

- [ ] ______
- [ ] ______
- [ ] ______
- [ ] ______
- [ ] ______

Wednesday

- [ ] ______
- [ ] ______
- [ ] ______
- [ ] ______
- [ ] ______

Thursday

- [ ] ______
- [ ] ______
- [ ] ______
- [ ] ______
- [ ] ______

Friday

- [ ] ______
- [ ] ______
- [ ] ______
- [ ] ______
- [ ] ______

Saturday

- [ ] ______
- [ ] ______
- [ ] ______
- [ ] ______
- [ ] ______

WEEK #2

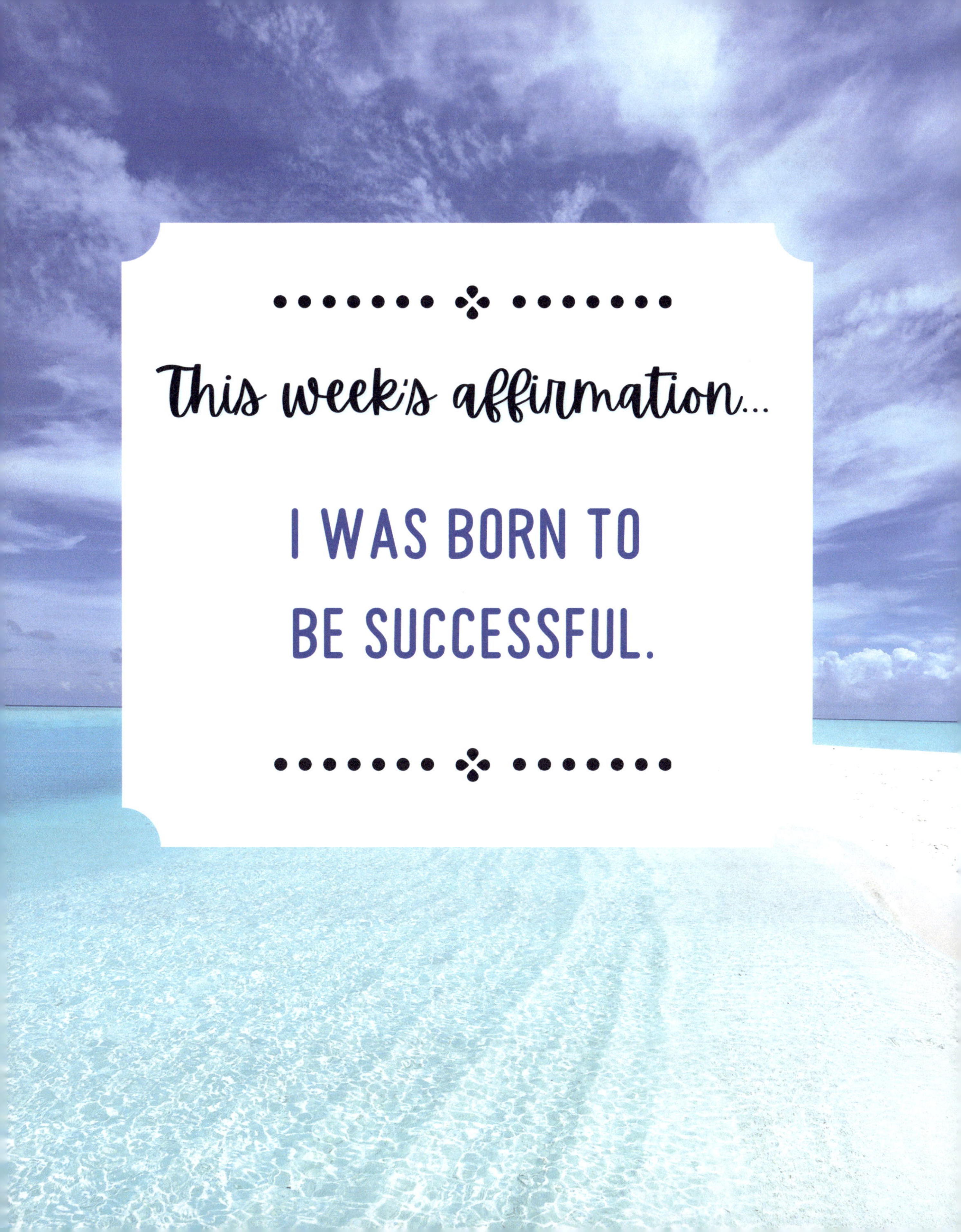
This week's affirmation...
I WAS BORN TO
BE SUCCESSFUL.

Weekly Goals Checklist

APRIL

List the steps you will take to complete your goal. Check off each step once complete.

WEEKLY FOCUS

Sunday

- ☐ __________
- ☐ __________
- ☐ __________
- ☐ __________
- ☐ __________

Monday

- ☐ __________
- ☐ __________
- ☐ __________
- ☐ __________
- ☐ __________

Tuesday

- ☐ __________
- ☐ __________
- ☐ __________
- ☐ __________
- ☐ __________

Wednesday

- ☐ __________
- ☐ __________
- ☐ __________
- ☐ __________
- ☐ __________

Thursday

- ☐ __________
- ☐ __________
- ☐ __________
- ☐ __________
- ☐ __________

Friday

- ☐ __________
- ☐ __________
- ☐ __________
- ☐ __________
- ☐ __________

Saturday

- ☐ __________
- ☐ __________
- ☐ __________
- ☐ __________
- ☐ __________

WEEK #3

This week's affirmation...

ALL THAT I WANT IN
LIFE IS WHAT
I DESERVE.

Weekly Goals Checklist

APRIL

List the steps you will take to complete your goal. Check off each step once complete.

WEEKLY FOCUS

Sunday

- [ ] ____________________
- [ ] ____________________
- [ ] ____________________
- [ ] ____________________
- [ ] ____________________

Monday

- [ ] ____________________
- [ ] ____________________
- [ ] ____________________
- [ ] ____________________
- [ ] ____________________

Tuesday

- [ ] ____________________
- [ ] ____________________
- [ ] ____________________
- [ ] ____________________
- [ ] ____________________

Wednesday

- [ ] ____________________
- [ ] ____________________
- [ ] ____________________
- [ ] ____________________
- [ ] ____________________

Thursday

- [ ] ____________________
- [ ] ____________________
- [ ] ____________________
- [ ] ____________________
- [ ] ____________________

Friday

- [ ] ____________________
- [ ] ____________________
- [ ] ____________________
- [ ] ____________________
- [ ] ____________________

Saturday

- [ ] ____________________
- [ ] ____________________
- [ ] ____________________
- [ ] ____________________
- [ ] ____________________

WEEK #4

This week's affirmation...

I ATTRACT SUCCESS,
HAPPINESS,
AND MONEY.

MAY

MONTH AT A GLANCE

"I AM ON THE PATHWAY TO FINANCIAL FREEDOM."

SUN	MON	TUE	WED	THURS	FRI	SAT

Notes:

Personal Vision Board

Date:

Visualize Your Month

Goals:

Financial:

To Buy:

Priorities:

Notes:

Weekly Goals Checklist

MAY

List the steps you will take to complete your goal. Check off each step once complete.

WEEKLY FOCUS

Sunday

- [ ] ______
- [ ] ______
- [ ] ______
- [ ] ______
- [ ] ______

Monday

- [ ] ______
- [ ] ______
- [ ] ______
- [ ] ______
- [ ] ______

Tuesday

- [ ] ______
- [ ] ______
- [ ] ______
- [ ] ______
- [ ] ______

Wednesday

- [ ] ______
- [ ] ______
- [ ] ______
- [ ] ______
- [ ] ______

Thursday

- [ ] ______
- [ ] ______
- [ ] ______
- [ ] ______
- [ ] ______

Friday

- [ ] ______
- [ ] ______
- [ ] ______
- [ ] ______
- [ ] ______

Saturday

- [ ] ______
- [ ] ______
- [ ] ______
- [ ] ______
- [ ] ______

WEEK #1

My Monthly DEBT LIST

Extra Payment To Put Towards Debt: ______________________________

Priority	Debt Name	Total Owed	Min. Monthly Pmt.	Extra Monthly Pmt.	Months To Pay Off

MONTHLY BILL TRACKER

Bill	Amount	Due Date	Paid

MONTHLY BUDGET SHEET

ESTIMATED BUDGET -

PRIORITIES -

BUDGET GOALS -

WAYS TO SAVE -

DESCRIPTION	BUDGET	SPENT

DESCRIPTION	BUDGET	SPENT

This week's affirmation...

I DESERVE TO CREATE
A LEGACY OF WEALTH
FOR MYSELF AND
MY FAMILY.

Weekly Goals Checklist

MAY

List the steps you will take to complete your goal. Check off each step once complete.

WEEKLY FOCUS

Sunday

- ■ ____________________
- ■ ____________________
- ■ ____________________
- ■ ____________________
- ■ ____________________

Monday

- ■ ____________________
- ■ ____________________
- ■ ____________________
- ■ ____________________
- ■ ____________________

Tuesday

- ■ ____________________
- ■ ____________________
- ■ ____________________
- ■ ____________________
- ■ ____________________

Wednesday

- ■ ____________________
- ■ ____________________
- ■ ____________________
- ■ ____________________
- ■ ____________________

Thursday

- ■ ____________________
- ■ ____________________
- ■ ____________________
- ■ ____________________
- ■ ____________________

Friday

- ■ ____________________
- ■ ____________________
- ■ ____________________
- ■ ____________________
- ■ ____________________

Saturday

- ■ ____________________
- ■ ____________________
- ■ ____________________
- ■ ____________________
- ■ ____________________

WEEK #2

This week's affirmation...

I WILL ACHIEVE FINANCIAL FREEDOM.

Weekly Goals Checklist

MAY

List the steps you will take to complete your goal. Check off each step once complete.

WEEKLY FOCUS

Sunday

- [ ] ____
- [ ] ____
- [ ] ____
- [ ] ____
- [ ] ____

Monday

- [ ] ____
- [ ] ____
- [ ] ____
- [ ] ____
- [ ] ____

Tuesday

- [ ] ____
- [ ] ____
- [ ] ____
- [ ] ____
- [ ] ____

Wednesday

- [ ] ____
- [ ] ____
- [ ] ____
- [ ] ____
- [ ] ____

Thursday

- [ ] ____
- [ ] ____
- [ ] ____
- [ ] ____
- [ ] ____

Friday

- [ ] ____
- [ ] ____
- [ ] ____
- [ ] ____
- [ ] ____

Saturday

- [ ] ____
- [ ] ____
- [ ] ____
- [ ] ____
- [ ] ____

WEEK #3

This week's affirmation...

MY FINANCES
WILL NOT
DEFEAT ME.

Weekly Goals Checklist

MAY

List the steps you will take to complete your goal. Check off each step once complete.

WEEKLY FOCUS

Sunday

- [ ] ______
- [ ] ______
- [ ] ______
- [ ] ______
- [ ] ______

Monday

- [ ] ______
- [ ] ______
- [ ] ______
- [ ] ______
- [ ] ______

Tuesday

- [ ] ______
- [ ] ______
- [ ] ______
- [ ] ______
- [ ] ______

Wednesday

- [ ] ______
- [ ] ______
- [ ] ______
- [ ] ______
- [ ] ______

Thursday

- [ ] ______
- [ ] ______
- [ ] ______
- [ ] ______
- [ ] ______

Friday

- [ ] ______
- [ ] ______
- [ ] ______
- [ ] ______
- [ ] ______

Saturday

- [ ] ______
- [ ] ______
- [ ] ______
- [ ] ______
- [ ] ______

WEEK #4

This week's affirmation...

I CAN REACH
ANY GOAL
I SET FOR MYSELF.

JUNE

MONTH AT A GLANCE

"I WILL CREATE A PLAN TO SAVE MONEY TODAY."

SUN	MON	TUE	WED	THURS	FRI	SAT

Notes:

Personal Vision Board

Date:

Visualize Your Month

Goals:

Financial:

To Buy:

Priorities:

Notes:

JUNE

Weekly Goals Checklist

List the steps you will take to complete your goal. Check off each step once complete.

WEEKLY FOCUS

Sunday

- [ ] ______
- [ ] ______
- [ ] ______
- [ ] ______
- [ ] ______

Monday

- [ ] ______
- [ ] ______
- [ ] ______
- [ ] ______
- [ ] ______

Tuesday

- [ ] ______
- [ ] ______
- [ ] ______
- [ ] ______
- [ ] ______

Wednesday

- [ ] ______
- [ ] ______
- [ ] ______
- [ ] ______
- [ ] ______

Thursday

- [ ] ______
- [ ] ______
- [ ] ______
- [ ] ______
- [ ] ______

Friday

- [ ] ______
- [ ] ______
- [ ] ______
- [ ] ______
- [ ] ______

Saturday

- [ ] ______
- [ ] ______
- [ ] ______
- [ ] ______
- [ ] ______

WEEK #1

My Monthly DEBT LIST

Extra Payment To Put Towards Debt: ______________________________

Priority	Debt Name	Total Owed	Min. Monthly Pmt.	Extra Monthly Pmt.	Months To Pay Off

MONTHLY BILL TRACKER

Bill	Amount	Due Date	Paid

MONTHLY BUDGET SHEET

ESTIMATED BUDGET -

PRIORITIES -

BUDGET GOALS -

WAYS TO SAVE -

DESCRIPTION	BUDGET	SPENT

DESCRIPTION	BUDGET	SPENT

This week's affirmation...

I WILL CONQUER ALL OF MY DEBT.

Weekly Goals Checklist

JUNE

List the steps you will take to complete your goal. Check off each step once complete.

WEEKLY FOCUS

Sunday

- ☐ ______
- ☐ ______
- ☐ ______
- ☐ ______
- ☐ ______

Monday

- ☐ ______
- ☐ ______
- ☐ ______
- ☐ ______
- ☐ ______

Tuesday

- ☐ ______
- ☐ ______
- ☐ ______
- ☐ ______
- ☐ ______

Wednesday

- ☐ ______
- ☐ ______
- ☐ ______
- ☐ ______
- ☐ ______

Thursday

- ☐ ______
- ☐ ______
- ☐ ______
- ☐ ______
- ☐ ______

Friday

- ☐ ______
- ☐ ______
- ☐ ______
- ☐ ______
- ☐ ______

Saturday

- ☐ ______
- ☐ ______
- ☐ ______
- ☐ ______
- ☐ ______

WEEK #2

This week's affirmation...

GOD HAS A FINANCIAL BLESSING WITH MY NAME ON IT.

Weekly Goals Checklist

JUNE

List the steps you will take to complete your goal. Check off each step once complete.

WEEKLY FOCUS	Sunday
	☐ ______
	☐ ______
	☐ ______
	☐ ______
	☐ ______

Monday	Tuesday
☐ ______	☐ ______
☐ ______	☐ ______
☐ ______	☐ ______
☐ ______	☐ ______
☐ ______	☐ ______

Wednesday	Thursday
☐ ______	☐ ______
☐ ______	☐ ______
☐ ______	☐ ______
☐ ______	☐ ______
☐ ______	☐ ______

Friday	Saturday
☐ ______	☐ ______
☐ ______	☐ ______
☐ ______	☐ ______
☐ ______	☐ ______
☐ ______	☐ ______

WEEK #3

This week's affirmation...

I HAVE THE RIGHT TO LIVE A DEBT FREE LIFE.

Weekly Goals Checklist

JUNE

List the steps you will take to complete your goal. Check off each step once complete.

WEEKLY FOCUS

Sunday

- [ ] ______
- [ ] ______
- [ ] ______
- [ ] ______
- [ ] ______

Monday

- [ ] ______
- [ ] ______
- [ ] ______
- [ ] ______
- [ ] ______

Tuesday

- [ ] ______
- [ ] ______
- [ ] ______
- [ ] ______
- [ ] ______

Wednesday

- [ ] ______
- [ ] ______
- [ ] ______
- [ ] ______
- [ ] ______

Thursday

- [ ] ______
- [ ] ______
- [ ] ______
- [ ] ______
- [ ] ______

Friday

- [ ] ______
- [ ] ______
- [ ] ______
- [ ] ______
- [ ] ______

Saturday

- [ ] ______
- [ ] ______
- [ ] ______
- [ ] ______
- [ ] ______

WEEK #4

This week's affirmation...

I SPEAK LIFE, WEALTH, HEALTH, AND PROSPERITY OVER MY LIFE.

JULY

MONTH AT A GLANCE

"I WILL NOT SPEND MONEY ON UNNECESSARY THINGS."

SUN	MON	TUE	WED	THURS	FRI	SAT

Notes:

Personal Vision Board

Date:

Visualize Your Month

Goals:

Financial:

To Buy:

Priorities:

Notes:

Weekly Goals Checklist

JULY

List the steps you will take to complete your goal. Check off each step once complete.

WEEKLY FOCUS

Sunday

- ■ ______
- ■ ______
- ■ ______
- ■ ______
- ■ ______

Monday

- ■ ______
- ■ ______
- ■ ______
- ■ ______
- ■ ______

Tuesday

- ■ ______
- ■ ______
- ■ ______
- ■ ______
- ■ ______

Wednesday

- ■ ______
- ■ ______
- ■ ______
- ■ ______
- ■ ______

Thursday

- ■ ______
- ■ ______
- ■ ______
- ■ ______
- ■ ______

Friday

- ■ ______
- ■ ______
- ■ ______
- ■ ______
- ■ ______

Saturday

- ■ ______
- ■ ______
- ■ ______
- ■ ______
- ■ ______

WEEK #1

My Monthly DEBT LIST

Extra Payment To Put Towards Debt: ____________________________

Priority	Debt Name	Total Owed	Min. Monthly Pmt.	Extra Monthly Pmt.	Months To Pay Off

MONTHLY BILL TRACKER

Bill	Amount	Due Date	Paid

MONTHLY BUDGET SHEET

ESTIMATED BUDGET -

PRIORITIES -

BUDGET GOALS -

WAYS TO SAVE -

DESCRIPTION	BUDGET	SPENT

DESCRIPTION	BUDGET	SPENT

This week's affirmation...

I WILL SET SMART GOALS TO ACHIEVE WHAT I WANT.

Weekly Goals Checklist

JULY

List the steps you will take to complete your goal. Check off each step once complete.

WEEKLY FOCUS

Sunday

- [ ] ______
- [ ] ______
- [ ] ______
- [ ] ______
- [ ] ______

Monday

- [ ] ______
- [ ] ______
- [ ] ______
- [ ] ______
- [ ] ______

Tuesday

- [ ] ______
- [ ] ______
- [ ] ______
- [ ] ______
- [ ] ______

Wednesday

- [ ] ______
- [ ] ______
- [ ] ______
- [ ] ______
- [ ] ______

Thursday

- [ ] ______
- [ ] ______
- [ ] ______
- [ ] ______
- [ ] ______

Friday

- [ ] ______
- [ ] ______
- [ ] ______
- [ ] ______
- [ ] ______

Saturday

- [ ] ______
- [ ] ______
- [ ] ______
- [ ] ______
- [ ] ______

WEEK #2

This week's affirmation...

I WON'T BE DISTRACTED BY OBSTACLES.

Weekly Goals Checklist

JULY

List the steps you will take to complete your goal. Check off each step once complete.

WEEKLY FOCUS

Sunday

- [ ] ____
- [ ] ____
- [ ] ____
- [ ] ____
- [ ] ____

Monday

- [ ] ____
- [ ] ____
- [ ] ____
- [ ] ____
- [ ] ____

Tuesday

- [ ] ____
- [ ] ____
- [ ] ____
- [ ] ____
- [ ] ____

Wednesday

- [ ] ____
- [ ] ____
- [ ] ____
- [ ] ____
- [ ] ____

Thursday

- [ ] ____
- [ ] ____
- [ ] ____
- [ ] ____
- [ ] ____

Friday

- [ ] ____
- [ ] ____
- [ ] ____
- [ ] ____
- [ ] ____

Saturday

- [ ] ____
- [ ] ____
- [ ] ____
- [ ] ____
- [ ] ____

WEEK #3

This week's affirmation...

MY FINANCIAL GOALS ARE A REALITY, NOT A DREAM.

Weekly Goals Checklist

JULY

List the steps you will take to complete your goal. Check off each step once complete.

WEEKLY FOCUS

Sunday

- [ ] ______
- [ ] ______
- [ ] ______
- [ ] ______
- [ ] ______

Monday

- [ ] ______
- [ ] ______
- [ ] ______
- [ ] ______
- [ ] ______

Tuesday

- [ ] ______
- [ ] ______
- [ ] ______
- [ ] ______
- [ ] ______

Wednesday

- [ ] ______
- [ ] ______
- [ ] ______
- [ ] ______
- [ ] ______

Thursday

- [ ] ______
- [ ] ______
- [ ] ______
- [ ] ______
- [ ] ______

Friday

- [ ] ______
- [ ] ______
- [ ] ______
- [ ] ______
- [ ] ______

Saturday

- [ ] ______
- [ ] ______
- [ ] ______
- [ ] ______
- [ ] ______

WEEK #4

This week's affirmation...

MONEY WILL OPEN
MORE DOORS AND
OPPORTUNITIES
FOR A FULFILLED LIFE.

AUGUST

MONTH AT A GLANCE

"I WILL ACHIEVE FINANCIAL FREEDOM."

SUN	MON	TUE	WED	THURS	FRI	SAT

Notes:

Personal Vision Board

Date:

Visualize Your Month

Goals:

Priorities:

Financial:

To Buy:

Notes:

AUGUST

Weekly Goals Checklist

List the steps you will take to complete your goal. Check off each step once complete.

WEEKLY FOCUS

Sunday

- [ ] ______
- [ ] ______
- [ ] ______
- [ ] ______
- [ ] ______

Monday

- [ ] ______
- [ ] ______
- [ ] ______
- [ ] ______
- [ ] ______

Tuesday

- [ ] ______
- [ ] ______
- [ ] ______
- [ ] ______
- [ ] ______

Wednesday

- [ ] ______
- [ ] ______
- [ ] ______
- [ ] ______
- [ ] ______

Thursday

- [ ] ______
- [ ] ______
- [ ] ______
- [ ] ______
- [ ] ______

Friday

- [ ] ______
- [ ] ______
- [ ] ______
- [ ] ______
- [ ] ______

Saturday

- [ ] ______
- [ ] ______
- [ ] ______
- [ ] ______
- [ ] ______

WEEK #1

My Monthly DEBT LIST

Extra Payment To Put Towards Debt: ______________________________

Priority	Debt Name	Total Owed	Min. Monthly Pmt.	Extra Monthly Pmt.	Months To Pay Off

MONTHLY BILL TRACKER

Bill	Amount	Due Date	Paid

MONTHLY BUDGET SHEET

ESTIMATED BUDGET -

BUDGET GOALS -

PRIORITIES -

WAYS TO SAVE -

DESCRIPTION	BUDGET	SPENT

DESCRIPTION	BUDGET	SPENT

This week's affirmation...

I WILL CREATE
A BUDGET AND
STICK TO IT.

Weekly Goals Checklist

AUGUST

List the steps you will take to complete your goal. Check off each step once complete.

WEEKLY FOCUS

Sunday

- [ ] ______
- [ ] ______
- [ ] ______
- [ ] ______
- [ ] ______

Monday

- [ ] ______
- [ ] ______
- [ ] ______
- [ ] ______
- [ ] ______

Tuesday

- [ ] ______
- [ ] ______
- [ ] ______
- [ ] ______
- [ ] ______

Wednesday

- [ ] ______
- [ ] ______
- [ ] ______
- [ ] ______
- [ ] ______

Thursday

- [ ] ______
- [ ] ______
- [ ] ______
- [ ] ______
- [ ] ______

Friday

- [ ] ______
- [ ] ______
- [ ] ______
- [ ] ______
- [ ] ______

Saturday

- [ ] ______
- [ ] ______
- [ ] ______
- [ ] ______
- [ ] ______

WEEK #2

This week's affirmation...

I WILL NOT BE AFFECTED BY NEGATIVE ATTITUDES.

AUGUST

Weekly Goals Checklist

List the steps you will take to complete your goal. Check off each step once complete.

WEEKLY FOCUS

Sunday

- [ ] ____
- [ ] ____
- [ ] ____
- [ ] ____
- [ ] ____

Monday

- [ ] ____
- [ ] ____
- [ ] ____
- [ ] ____
- [ ] ____

Tuesday

- [ ] ____
- [ ] ____
- [ ] ____
- [ ] ____
- [ ] ____

Wednesday

- [ ] ____
- [ ] ____
- [ ] ____
- [ ] ____
- [ ] ____

Thursday

- [ ] ____
- [ ] ____
- [ ] ____
- [ ] ____
- [ ] ____

Friday

- [ ] ____
- [ ] ____
- [ ] ____
- [ ] ____
- [ ] ____

Saturday

- [ ] ____
- [ ] ____
- [ ] ____
- [ ] ____
- [ ] ____

WEEK #3

This week's affirmation...

I WILL COMMIT TO INVESTING IN MY FUTURE.

Weekly Goals Checklist

AUGUST

List the steps you will take to complete your goal. Check off each step once complete.

WEEKLY FOCUS

Sunday

- ☐ ____
- ☐ ____
- ☐ ____
- ☐ ____
- ☐ ____

Monday

- ☐ ____
- ☐ ____
- ☐ ____
- ☐ ____
- ☐ ____

Tuesday

- ☐ ____
- ☐ ____
- ☐ ____
- ☐ ____
- ☐ ____

Wednesday

- ☐ ____
- ☐ ____
- ☐ ____
- ☐ ____
- ☐ ____

Thursday

- ☐ ____
- ☐ ____
- ☐ ____
- ☐ ____
- ☐ ____

Friday

- ☐ ____
- ☐ ____
- ☐ ____
- ☐ ____
- ☐ ____

Saturday

- ☐ ____
- ☐ ____
- ☐ ____
- ☐ ____
- ☐ ____

WEEK #4

This week's affirmation...
SAVING MONEY
COMES NATURALLY.

SEPTEMBER

MONTH AT A GLANCE

"I WILL STICK TO MY BUDGET."

SUN	MON	TUE	WED	THURS	FRI	SAT

Notes:

Personal Vision Board

Date:

Visualize Your Month

Goals:

Financial:

To Buy:

Priorities:

Notes:

Weekly Goals Checklist

SEPTEMBER

List the steps you will take to complete your goal. Check off each step once complete.

WEEKLY FOCUS

Sunday

- [ ] ______
- [ ] ______
- [ ] ______
- [ ] ______
- [ ] ______

Monday

- [ ] ______
- [ ] ______
- [ ] ______
- [ ] ______
- [ ] ______

Tuesday

- [ ] ______
- [ ] ______
- [ ] ______
- [ ] ______
- [ ] ______

Wednesday

- [ ] ______
- [ ] ______
- [ ] ______
- [ ] ______
- [ ] ______

Thursday

- [ ] ______
- [ ] ______
- [ ] ______
- [ ] ______
- [ ] ______

Friday

- [ ] ______
- [ ] ______
- [ ] ______
- [ ] ______
- [ ] ______

Saturday

- [ ] ______
- [ ] ______
- [ ] ______
- [ ] ______
- [ ] ______

My Monthly DEBT LIST

Extra Payment To Put Towards Debt: ______________________

Priority	Debt Name	Total Owed	Min. Monthly Pmt.	Extra Monthly Pmt.	Months To Pay Off

MONTHLY BILL TRACKER

Bill	Amount	Due Date	Paid

MONTHLY BUDGET SHEET

ESTIMATED BUDGET -

PRIORITIES -

BUDGET GOALS -

WAYS TO SAVE -

DESCRIPTION	BUDGET	SPENT

DESCRIPTION	BUDGET	SPENT

This week's affirmation...

I WILL SET
A DUE DATE
FOR GOALS TODAY.

Weekly Goals Checklist

SEPTEMBER

List the steps you will take to complete your goal. Check off each step once complete.

WEEKLY FOCUS

Sunday

- [ ] ____
- [ ] ____
- [ ] ____
- [ ] ____
- [ ] ____

Monday

- [ ] ____
- [ ] ____
- [ ] ____
- [ ] ____
- [ ] ____

Tuesday

- [ ] ____
- [ ] ____
- [ ] ____
- [ ] ____
- [ ] ____

Wednesday

- [ ] ____
- [ ] ____
- [ ] ____
- [ ] ____
- [ ] ____

Thursday

- [ ] ____
- [ ] ____
- [ ] ____
- [ ] ____
- [ ] ____

Friday

- [ ] ____
- [ ] ____
- [ ] ____
- [ ] ____
- [ ] ____

Saturday

- [ ] ____
- [ ] ____
- [ ] ____
- [ ] ____
- [ ] ____

WEEK #2

This week's affirmation...
I AM A MAGNET
FOR MONEY.

Weekly Goals Checklist

SEPTEMBER

List the steps you will take to complete your goal. Check off each step once complete.

WEEKLY FOCUS

Sunday

- [ ] ____________________
- [ ] ____________________
- [ ] ____________________
- [ ] ____________________
- [ ] ____________________

Monday

- [ ] ____________________
- [ ] ____________________
- [ ] ____________________
- [ ] ____________________
- [ ] ____________________

Tuesday

- [ ] ____________________
- [ ] ____________________
- [ ] ____________________
- [ ] ____________________
- [ ] ____________________

Wednesday

- [ ] ____________________
- [ ] ____________________
- [ ] ____________________
- [ ] ____________________
- [ ] ____________________

Thursday

- [ ] ____________________
- [ ] ____________________
- [ ] ____________________
- [ ] ____________________
- [ ] ____________________

Friday

- [ ] ____________________
- [ ] ____________________
- [ ] ____________________
- [ ] ____________________
- [ ] ____________________

Saturday

- [ ] ____________________
- [ ] ____________________
- [ ] ____________________
- [ ] ____________________
- [ ] ____________________

WEEK #3

This week's affirmation...

I AM CAPABLE OF SETTING REALISTIC GOALS.

Weekly Goals Checklist

SEPTEMBER

List the steps you will take to complete your goal. Check off each step once complete.

WEEKLY FOCUS

Sunday

- ☐ ____________________
- ☐ ____________________
- ☐ ____________________
- ☐ ____________________
- ☐ ____________________

Monday

- ☐ ____________________
- ☐ ____________________
- ☐ ____________________
- ☐ ____________________
- ☐ ____________________

Tuesday

- ☐ ____________________
- ☐ ____________________
- ☐ ____________________
- ☐ ____________________
- ☐ ____________________

Wednesday

- ☐ ____________________
- ☐ ____________________
- ☐ ____________________
- ☐ ____________________
- ☐ ____________________

Thursday

- ☐ ____________________
- ☐ ____________________
- ☐ ____________________
- ☐ ____________________
- ☐ ____________________

Friday

- ☐ ____________________
- ☐ ____________________
- ☐ ____________________
- ☐ ____________________
- ☐ ____________________

Saturday

- ☐ ____________________
- ☐ ____________________
- ☐ ____________________
- ☐ ____________________
- ☐ ____________________

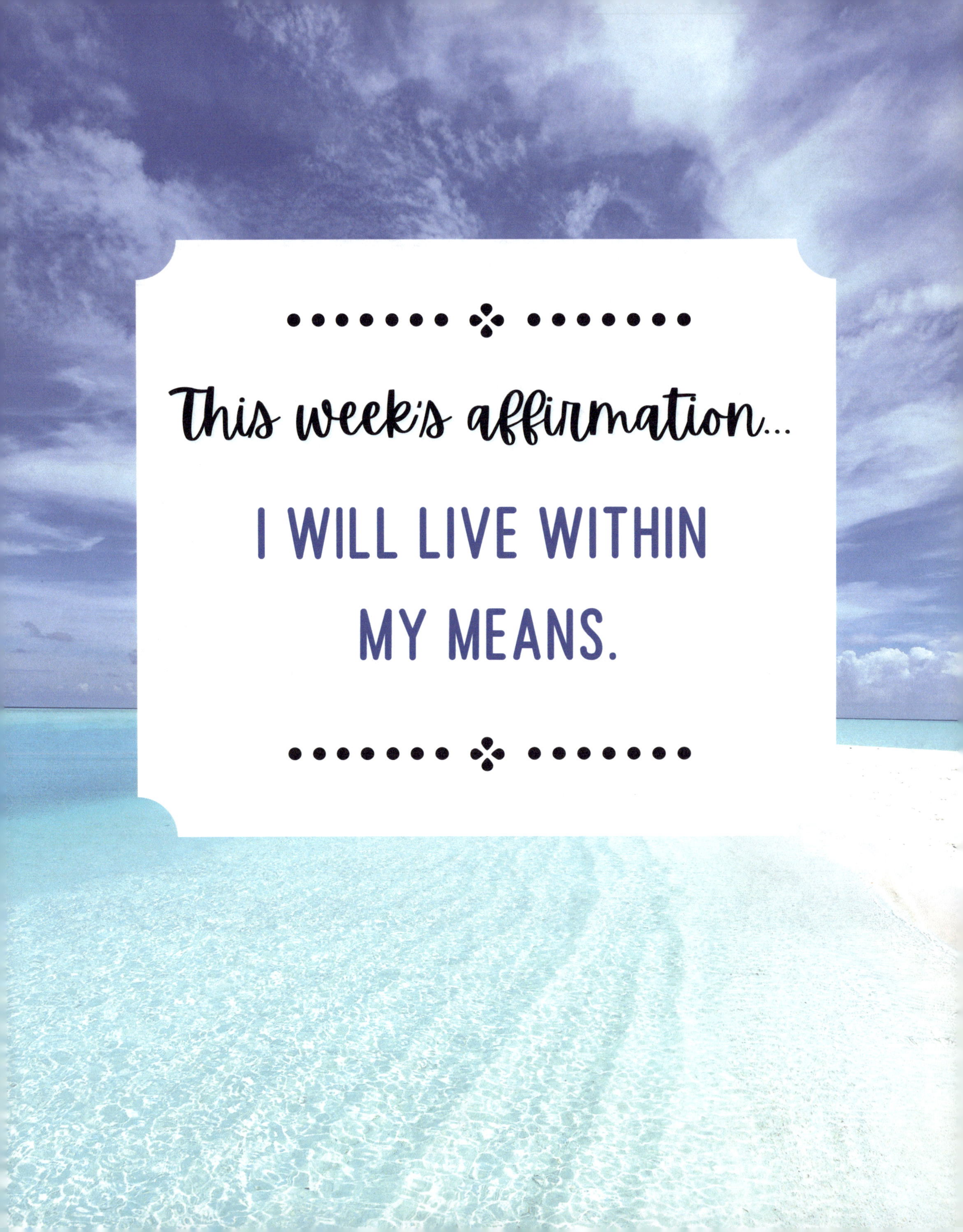

This week's affirmation…

I WILL LIVE WITHIN MY MEANS.

OCTOBER

MONTH AT A GLANCE

"I WILL LIVE A DEBT FREE LIFE."

SUN	MON	TUE	WED	THURS	FRI	SAT

Notes:

Personal Vision Board

Date:

Visualize Your Month

Goals:

Priorities:

Financial:

To Buy:

Notes:

Weekly Goals Checklist

OCTOBER

List the steps you will take to complete your goal. Check off each step once complete.

WEEKLY FOCUS

Sunday

- ☐ ____
- ☐ ____
- ☐ ____
- ☐ ____
- ☐ ____

Monday

- ☐ ____
- ☐ ____
- ☐ ____
- ☐ ____
- ☐ ____

Tuesday

- ☐ ____
- ☐ ____
- ☐ ____
- ☐ ____
- ☐ ____

Wednesday

- ☐ ____
- ☐ ____
- ☐ ____
- ☐ ____
- ☐ ____

Thursday

- ☐ ____
- ☐ ____
- ☐ ____
- ☐ ____
- ☐ ____

Friday

- ☐ ____
- ☐ ____
- ☐ ____
- ☐ ____
- ☐ ____

Saturday

- ☐ ____
- ☐ ____
- ☐ ____
- ☐ ____
- ☐ ____

WEEK #1

My Monthly DEBT LIST

Extra Payment To Put Towards Debt: ____________________________

Priority	Debt Name	Total Owed	Min. Monthly Pmt.	Extra Monthly Pmt.	Months To Pay Off

MONTHLY BILL TRACKER

Bill	Amount	Due Date	Paid

MONTHLY BUDGET SHEET

ESTIMATED BUDGET -

PRIORITIES -

BUDGET GOALS -

WAYS TO SAVE -

DESCRIPTION	BUDGET	SPENT

DESCRIPTION	BUDGET	SPENT

This week's affirmation...

I LIKE SETTING CHALLENGING GOALS.

Weekly Goals Checklist

OCTOBER

List the steps you will take to complete your goal. Check off each step once complete.

WEEKLY FOCUS

Sunday

- [ ] ____________________
- [ ] ____________________
- [ ] ____________________
- [ ] ____________________
- [ ] ____________________

Monday

- [ ] ____________________
- [ ] ____________________
- [ ] ____________________
- [ ] ____________________
- [ ] ____________________

Tuesday

- [ ] ____________________
- [ ] ____________________
- [ ] ____________________
- [ ] ____________________
- [ ] ____________________

Wednesday

- [ ] ____________________
- [ ] ____________________
- [ ] ____________________
- [ ] ____________________
- [ ] ____________________

Thursday

- [ ] ____________________
- [ ] ____________________
- [ ] ____________________
- [ ] ____________________
- [ ] ____________________

Friday

- [ ] ____________________
- [ ] ____________________
- [ ] ____________________
- [ ] ____________________
- [ ] ____________________

Saturday

- [ ] ____________________
- [ ] ____________________
- [ ] ____________________
- [ ] ____________________
- [ ] ____________________

WEEK #2

This week's affirmation...

I AM EXCITED TO
ACHIEVE MY
FINANCIAL GOALS.

Weekly Goals Checklist

OCTOBER

List the steps you will take to complete your goal. Check off each step once complete.

WEEKLY FOCUS

Sunday

- [ ] ______
- [ ] ______
- [ ] ______
- [ ] ______
- [ ] ______

Monday

- [ ] ______
- [ ] ______
- [ ] ______
- [ ] ______
- [ ] ______

Tuesday

- [ ] ______
- [ ] ______
- [ ] ______
- [ ] ______
- [ ] ______

Wednesday

- [ ] ______
- [ ] ______
- [ ] ______
- [ ] ______
- [ ] ______

Thursday

- [ ] ______
- [ ] ______
- [ ] ______
- [ ] ______
- [ ] ______

Friday

- [ ] ______
- [ ] ______
- [ ] ______
- [ ] ______
- [ ] ______

Saturday

- [ ] ______
- [ ] ______
- [ ] ______
- [ ] ______
- [ ] ______

WEEK #3

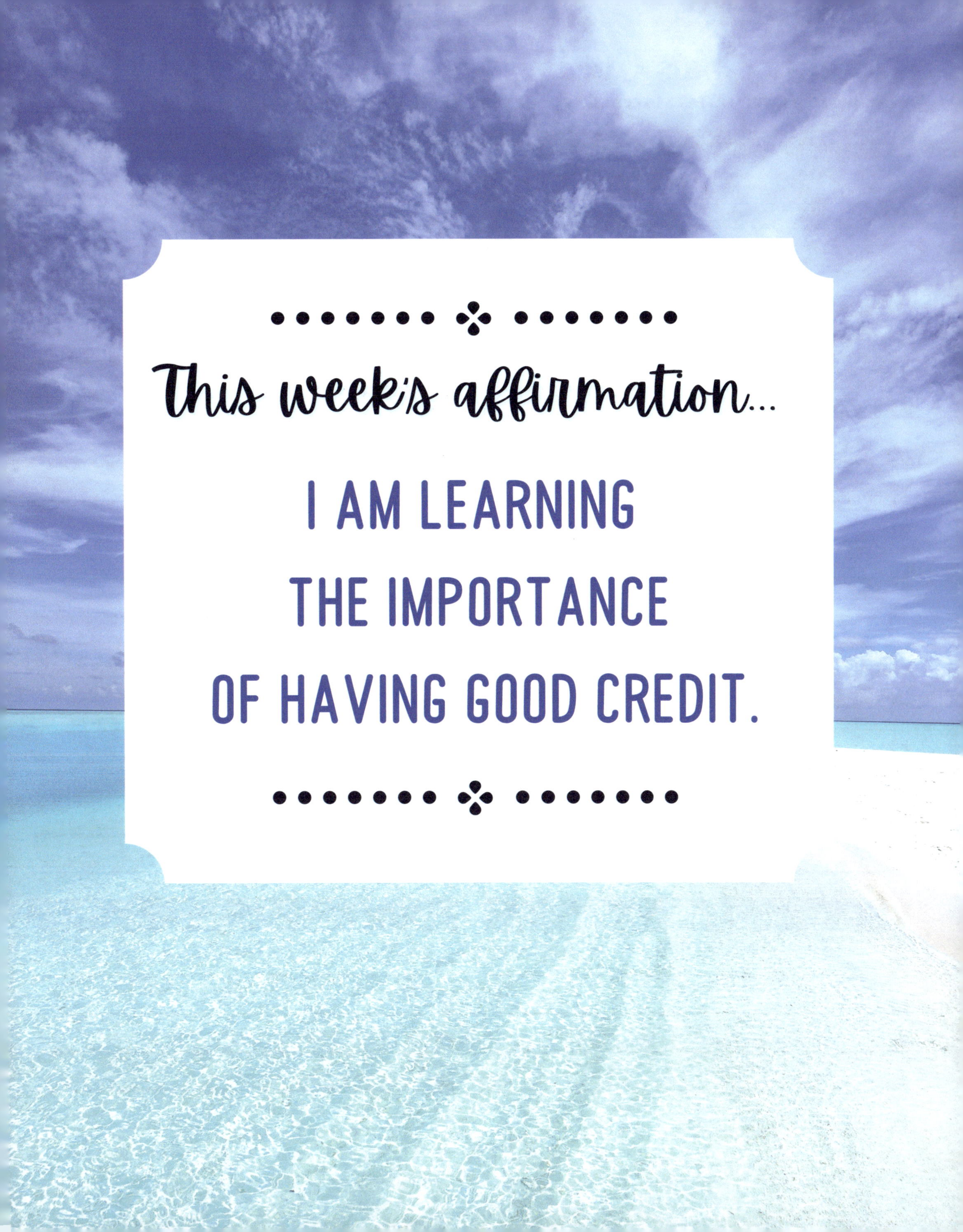

This week's affirmation...

I AM LEARNING THE IMPORTANCE OF HAVING GOOD CREDIT.

Weekly Goals Checklist

OCTOBER

List the steps you will take to complete your goal. Check off each step once complete.

WEEKLY FOCUS

Sunday

- [ ] ______
- [ ] ______
- [ ] ______
- [ ] ______
- [ ] ______

Monday

- [ ] ______
- [ ] ______
- [ ] ______
- [ ] ______
- [ ] ______

Tuesday

- [ ] ______
- [ ] ______
- [ ] ______
- [ ] ______
- [ ] ______

Wednesday

- [ ] ______
- [ ] ______
- [ ] ______
- [ ] ______
- [ ] ______

Thursday

- [ ] ______
- [ ] ______
- [ ] ______
- [ ] ______
- [ ] ______

Friday

- [ ] ______
- [ ] ______
- [ ] ______
- [ ] ______
- [ ] ______

Saturday

- [ ] ______
- [ ] ______
- [ ] ______
- [ ] ______
- [ ] ______

This week's affirmation...

I WILL NOT SPEND OUTSIDE OF MY BUDGET.

NOVEMBER

MONTH AT A GLANCE

"I SPEAK PEACE AND FINANCIAL FREEDOM OVER MY LIFE."

SUN	MON	TUE	WED	THURS	FRI	SAT

Notes:

Personal Vision Board

Date:

Visualize Your Month

Goals:

Financial:

To Buy:

Priorities:

Notes:

Weekly Goals Checklist

NOVEMBER

List the steps you will take to complete your goal. Check off each step once complete.

WEEKLY FOCUS

Sunday

- [ ] ______
- [ ] ______
- [ ] ______
- [ ] ______
- [ ] ______

Monday

- [ ] ______
- [ ] ______
- [ ] ______
- [ ] ______
- [ ] ______

Tuesday

- [ ] ______
- [ ] ______
- [ ] ______
- [ ] ______
- [ ] ______

Wednesday

- [ ] ______
- [ ] ______
- [ ] ______
- [ ] ______
- [ ] ______

Thursday

- [ ] ______
- [ ] ______
- [ ] ______
- [ ] ______
- [ ] ______

Friday

- [ ] ______
- [ ] ______
- [ ] ______
- [ ] ______
- [ ] ______

Saturday

- [ ] ______
- [ ] ______
- [ ] ______
- [ ] ______
- [ ] ______

WEEK #1

My Monthly DEBT LIST

Extra Payment To Put Towards Debt: ______________________________

Priority	Debt Name	Total Owed	Min. Monthly Pmt.	Extra Monthly Pmt.	Months To Pay Off

MONTHLY BILL TRACKER

Bill	Amount	Due Date	Paid

MONTHLY BUDGET SHEET

ESTIMATED BUDGET -

PRIORITIES -

BUDGET GOALS -

WAYS TO SAVE -

DESCRIPTION	BUDGET	SPENT

DESCRIPTION	BUDGET	SPENT

This week's affirmation...

I DESERVE TO SET MYSELF UP FOR SUCCESS.

Weekly Goals Checklist

NOVEMBER

List the steps you will take to complete your goal. Check off each step once complete.

WEEKLY FOCUS

Sunday

- ☐ ____
- ☐ ____
- ☐ ____
- ☐ ____
- ☐ ____

Monday

- ☐ ____
- ☐ ____
- ☐ ____
- ☐ ____
- ☐ ____

Tuesday

- ☐ ____
- ☐ ____
- ☐ ____
- ☐ ____
- ☐ ____

Wednesday

- ☐ ____
- ☐ ____
- ☐ ____
- ☐ ____
- ☐ ____

Thursday

- ☐ ____
- ☐ ____
- ☐ ____
- ☐ ____
- ☐ ____

Friday

- ☐ ____
- ☐ ____
- ☐ ____
- ☐ ____
- ☐ ____

Saturday

- ☐ ____
- ☐ ____
- ☐ ____
- ☐ ____
- ☐ ____

WEEK #2

This week's affirmation...

I DO NOT HAVE TO LIVE PAYCHECK TO PAYCHECK.

Weekly Goals Checklist

NOVEMBER

List the steps you will take to complete your goal. Check off each step once complete.

WEEKLY FOCUS

Sunday

- [ ] ____
- [ ] ____
- [ ] ____
- [ ] ____
- [ ] ____

Monday

- [ ] ____
- [ ] ____
- [ ] ____
- [ ] ____
- [ ] ____

Tuesday

- [ ] ____
- [ ] ____
- [ ] ____
- [ ] ____
- [ ] ____

Wednesday

- [ ] ____
- [ ] ____
- [ ] ____
- [ ] ____
- [ ] ____

Thursday

- [ ] ____
- [ ] ____
- [ ] ____
- [ ] ____
- [ ] ____

Friday

- [ ] ____
- [ ] ____
- [ ] ____
- [ ] ____
- [ ] ____

Saturday

- [ ] ____
- [ ] ____
- [ ] ____
- [ ] ____
- [ ] ____

WEEK #3

This week's affirmation...

I WILL RESEARCH THE BEST RETIREMENT SAVINGS PLAN FOR ME.

Weekly Goals Checklist

NOVEMBER

List the steps you will take to complete your goal. Check off each step once complete.

WEEKLY FOCUS

Sunday

Monday

Tuesday

Wednesday

Thursday

Friday

Saturday

WEEK #4

This week's affirmation...

I DESERVE TO HAVE A FINANCIAL FOUNDATION BUILT ON WEALTH.

DECEMBER

MONTH AT A GLANCE

"I WILL FINISH WHAT I STARTED."

SUN	MON	TUE	WED	THURS	FRI	SAT

Notes:

Personal Vision Board

Date:

Visualize Your Month

Goals:

Priorities:

Financial:

To Buy:

Notes:

Weekly Goals Checklist

DECEMBER

List the steps you will take to complete your goal. Check off each step once complete.

WEEKLY FOCUS

Sunday

- [ ] ______
- [ ] ______
- [ ] ______
- [ ] ______
- [ ] ______

Monday

- [ ] ______
- [ ] ______
- [ ] ______
- [ ] ______
- [ ] ______

Tuesday

- [ ] ______
- [ ] ______
- [ ] ______
- [ ] ______
- [ ] ______

Wednesday

- [ ] ______
- [ ] ______
- [ ] ______
- [ ] ______
- [ ] ______

Thursday

- [ ] ______
- [ ] ______
- [ ] ______
- [ ] ______
- [ ] ______

Friday

- [ ] ______
- [ ] ______
- [ ] ______
- [ ] ______
- [ ] ______

Saturday

- [ ] ______
- [ ] ______
- [ ] ______
- [ ] ______
- [ ] ______

WEEK #1

My Monthly DEBT LIST

Extra Payment To Put Towards Debt: ______________________________

Priority	Debt Name	Total Owed	Min. Monthly Pmt.	Extra Monthly Pmt.	Months To Pay Off

MONTHLY BILL TRACKER

Bill	Amount	Due Date	Paid

MONTHLY BUDGET SHEET

ESTIMATED BUDGET -

PRIORITIES -

BUDGET GOALS -

WAYS TO SAVE -

DESCRIPTION	BUDGET	SPENT

DESCRIPTION	BUDGET	SPENT

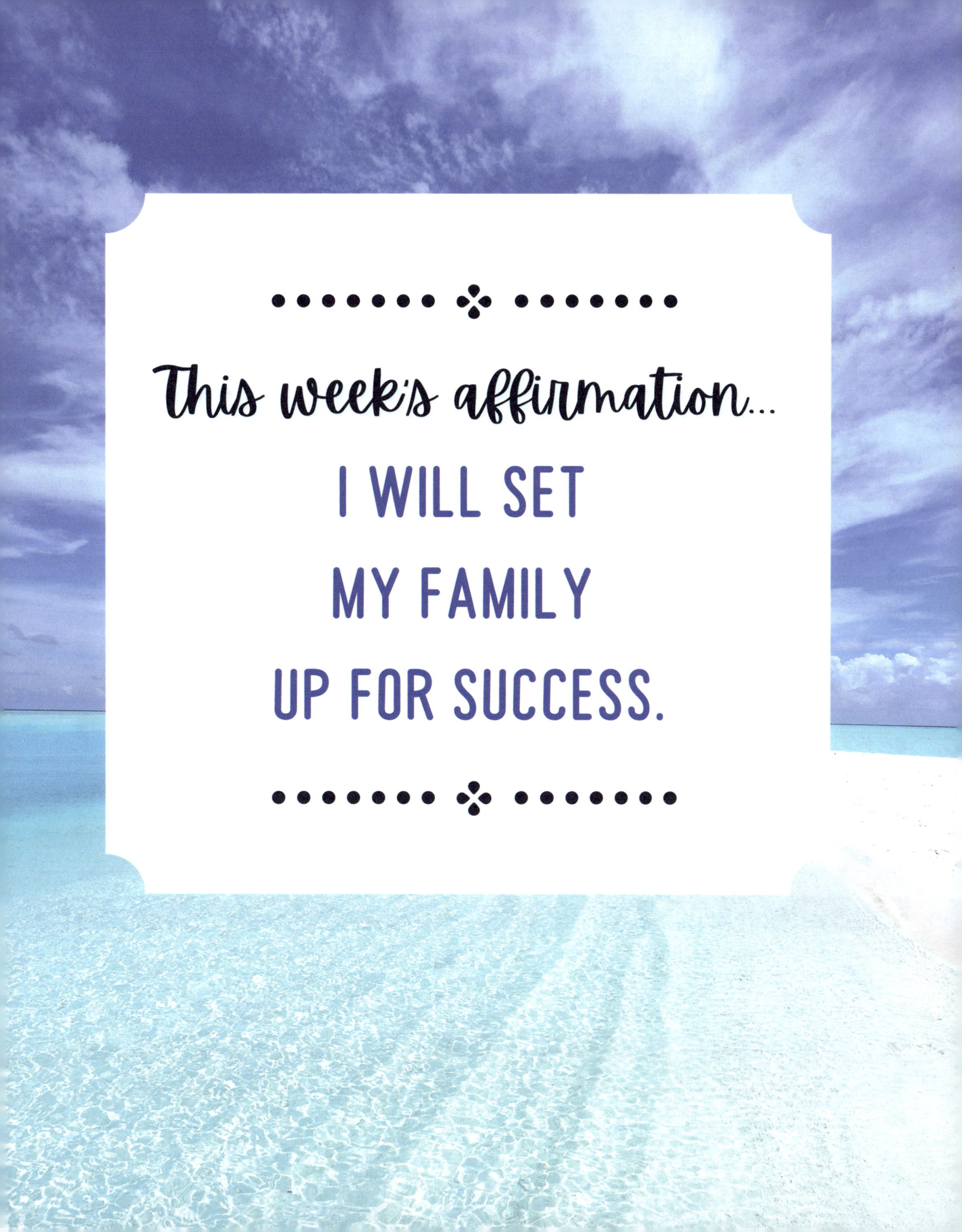

This week's affirmation...

I WILL SET MY FAMILY UP FOR SUCCESS.

Weekly Goals Checklist

DECEMBER

List the steps you will take to complete your goal. Check off each step once complete.

WEEKLY FOCUS

Sunday

- [ ] ______
- [ ] ______
- [ ] ______
- [ ] ______
- [ ] ______

Monday

- [ ] ______
- [ ] ______
- [ ] ______
- [ ] ______
- [ ] ______

Tuesday

- [ ] ______
- [ ] ______
- [ ] ______
- [ ] ______
- [ ] ______

Wednesday

- [ ] ______
- [ ] ______
- [ ] ______
- [ ] ______
- [ ] ______

Thursday

- [ ] ______
- [ ] ______
- [ ] ______
- [ ] ______
- [ ] ______

Friday

- [ ] ______
- [ ] ______
- [ ] ______
- [ ] ______
- [ ] ______

Saturday

- [ ] ______
- [ ] ______
- [ ] ______
- [ ] ______
- [ ] ______

WEEK #2

This week's affirmation...

I AM CONFIDENT
IN MY ABILITY
TO LEARN NEW
IDEAS ABOUT MONEY.

Weekly Goals Checklist

DECEMBER

List the steps you will take to complete your goal. Check off each step once complete.

WEEKLY FOCUS

Sunday

- [ ] ____
- [ ] ____
- [ ] ____
- [ ] ____
- [ ] ____

Monday

- [ ] ____
- [ ] ____
- [ ] ____
- [ ] ____
- [ ] ____

Tuesday

- [ ] ____
- [ ] ____
- [ ] ____
- [ ] ____
- [ ] ____

Wednesday

- [ ] ____
- [ ] ____
- [ ] ____
- [ ] ____
- [ ] ____

Thursday

- [ ] ____
- [ ] ____
- [ ] ____
- [ ] ____
- [ ] ____

Friday

- [ ] ____
- [ ] ____
- [ ] ____
- [ ] ____
- [ ] ____

Saturday

- [ ] ____
- [ ] ____
- [ ] ____
- [ ] ____
- [ ] ____

WEEK #3

This week's affirmation...

I WILL BE PATIENT IN MY FINANCIAL JOURNEY.

Weekly Goals Checklist

DECEMBER

List the steps you will take to complete your goal. Check off each step once complete.

WEEKLY FOCUS

Sunday

- ☐ ____
- ☐ ____
- ☐ ____
- ☐ ____
- ☐ ____

Monday

- ☐ ____
- ☐ ____
- ☐ ____
- ☐ ____
- ☐ ____

Tuesday

- ☐ ____
- ☐ ____
- ☐ ____
- ☐ ____
- ☐ ____

Wednesday

- ☐ ____
- ☐ ____
- ☐ ____
- ☐ ____
- ☐ ____

Thursday

- ☐ ____
- ☐ ____
- ☐ ____
- ☐ ____
- ☐ ____

Friday

- ☐ ____
- ☐ ____
- ☐ ____
- ☐ ____
- ☐ ____

Saturday

- ☐ ____
- ☐ ____
- ☐ ____
- ☐ ____
- ☐ ____

WEEK #4

This week's affirmation...

I WILL WORK HARD TO ACHIEVE EVERY FINANCIAL GOAL I SET.

NOTES

NOTES

NOTES

NOTES

NOTES

NOTES

NOTES

NOTES

NOTES

NOTES

NOTES

NOTES

NOTES

NOTES

NOTES

MEET THE AUTHOR

SELENA GIBBONS

Selena helps working professionals,
college students, single mother's,
married couples, and entrepreneurs
find peace and structure
as they build and organize a plan
towards financial freedom.

CONTACT THE AUTHOR

Website:

www.selenagibbons.com

Business Phone:

1-786-383-4257

Email:

financialfreedom@selenagibbons.com

Facebook:

800+ Financial Freedom Club

Podcast:

800+ Financial Freedom Podcast

Other Books By The Author

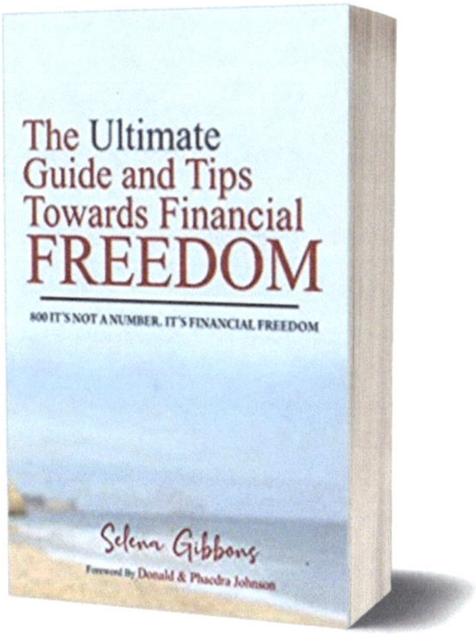

Have you ever lived Paycheck to Paycheck? Are you ready to get out of debt? Fear not there is still HOPE and help available to you with this book "The Ultimate Guide and Tips Towards Financial Freedom." This book is filled with all the tools and resources that you will need to help you reach your financial goals.

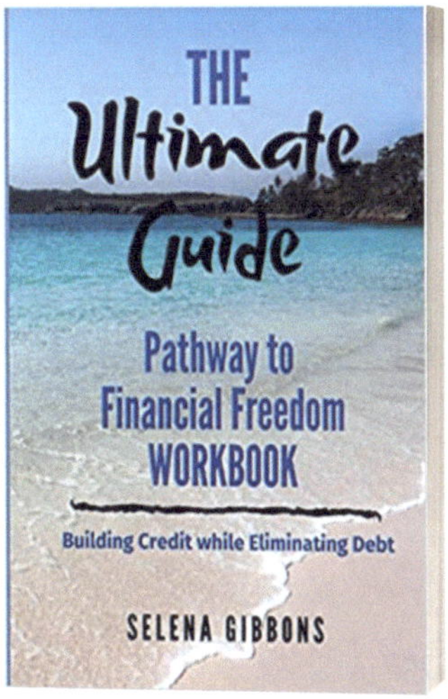

This action packed workbook is a follow up to my Book: The Ultimate Guide-Tips towards Financial Freedom. After getting such great feedback from readers on how the book was helping their credit building efforts, I took the time to develop this workbook, which accompanies my online credit building course.

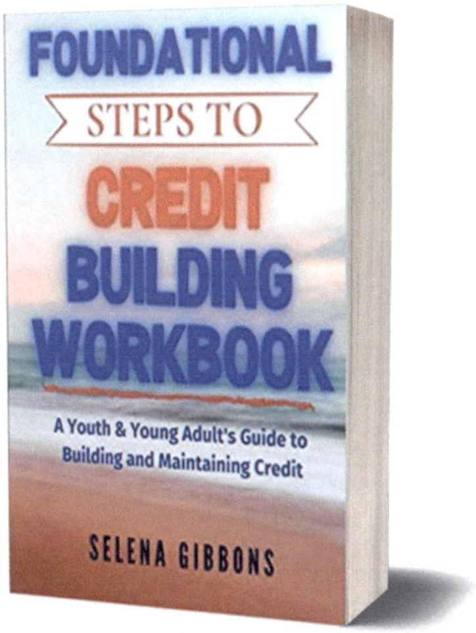

Starting out in life on the right track financially can be challenging. That is why I developed this workbook to help you navigate early in life. If you start out with the right habits, you will maintain a good foundation in which to build upon. It's never too early to start out strong!

Made in the USA
Monee, IL
05 November 2026

67808873R00098